THE MAGPIE

AND OTHER POEMS OF LOVE, ART AND INSANITY

AL MINAR M. REZA

For Sir Asok Kumar Dutta

Contents

Preface *ix*

Acknowledgements *xi*

Part 1

1. Broken Oaths 3
2. The Maiden I Dreamt About 4
3. The Last Bullet 6
4. Our Flowers 8
5. How Rich The Earth Is 11
6. The Magpie 12
7. To Die By Your Hands 16
8. The Black Box 17
9. The Valley Of Dead 20
10. Midnight Moth 21

Part 2

11. The Visit 27
12. To Art Is To Sin 29
13. The Blood Painter 32
14. Funeral Mutation 35
15. The Wall 38
16. The Mermaid 42
17. The Chair Of Lazarus 47
18. The Weeping Statue 54
19. Hands Of A Poet 60
20. The Scientist 65

Contents

Part 3

21. What Memory Holds 73
22. A Hypocite's Poem 74
23. Villains 77
24. When 79
25. Thy 81
26. When God Cried 82
27. Fools And Intellects 84
28. The Sparrow That Flew Away 85
29. Death Greets Life 86
30. Blind Eyes 88

Part 4

31. If Love Could Bleed 93
32. Love Is Worship 94
33. Below The Earth 95
34. Goldfinch 96
35. The Song Of Your Ribs 98
36. Lost Memory 99
37. Rebels 100
38. Youth 102
39. Mother Of All Poets 103
40. About You 104

NOTES 105

BIBLIOGRAPHY 113

This book is a collection of forty poems divided into four parts: Death, Resurrection, Redemption, and Love. It consists of poems which unreliable narrators, gothic elements, the grotesque side of human metaphysics, insanity, art, and love. The readers will be forced to feel uneasy and unhinged as the spine-chilling poems take eerie turns- for better and for worse. But we shall venture beyond the insanity to seek love and harmony. We shall venture into a world of tragic and dark happenings, a world of the living dead, where the spirits shall enchant us with their tales and macabre pasts.

Preface

Why shall I write about things that do not make sense, and why shall my writings ever make any sense?

Acknowledgements

I would like to show my gratitude towards my mother, for whom I am forever in debt. I acknowledge the support and cooperation of my mentor, Sir Asok Kumar Dutta, and my creative friend, Samriddhi Chakraborty, who have read each one of my poems and helped me with the editing process.

AL MINAR M. REZA

The Magpie

And Other Poems Of Love, Art, and Insanity.

"Extremum vitae spiritum edere"

DEATH

1. Broken Oaths

For the winters morrow,
Today, too, snow beruffled my heart.
For the woods so deep and narrow,
Today, too, I lost myself on the Earth.

.

For the desolated deserts of darkness,
Today, too, you rest below the Earth.
For the night's blind winds whisper loneliness,
Today, too, I search for you among the stars.

.

Today, too, our broken Oaths spoil my dreams,
Today, too, the tainted heart of mine screams.

2. The Maiden I Dreamt About

Years of solitary, away from my childhood, I spent,
With a letter on my hand which was sent
By someone I didn't know from my reality but in my dreams
She was the spring who bewitched my soul— as it seems
The Earth, itself, had dressed
As a woman of ethereal virtues.

.

From the stillness of this life, I venture far beyond
In search of the lady who sought my dreams so gaunt—
Like the midnight tides seek for the shore.
She's a being, a nonpareil maiden of forevermore,
With an abyss in her eyes that echoed elegies,
Which could give life to those vicious effigies.

.

The Maiden I dreamt about lives beyond the known lands,
Or mountains, or oceans made up of mere sands.
She lives and waits, for me, like the stormy night
Waits for the wild kisses of the thunders so bright.

.

The Maiden I dreamt about would close my eyes,
Like the young sky greets the visiting sunrise,
For there are no hopeful convictions left in me—

For my life never became what it meant to be
Because I was a poet who could never write poetry;
And I wish my life was something more than a tragedy.

.

Oh, the Maiden of my dreams!
God made you before He made me—
I could feel your tender hands wrapping me.
No matter how twisted the words of unwise mortals are;
I know you can never be a demon from afar.
But I've nothing to offer you than my poetry—
Why'd you measure our love
In exchange for my life of insanity?

.

Though I loved her every fathom of time, I loathe her now
For to be with her, she demands a lot in one vow;
That I must leave behind everything I am,
That I must stop pondering everything I could be
Because the name of the Maiden I dreamt about is *Death*
And she waited nameless eternities for me.

3. The Last Bullet

Seven bullets, one gun
With a dreadful hound.
Soaked in blood, from head to toes,
The chaos inside and outside;
Death is laughing at us, I suppose.

.

After the gunpowder smell,
Glorious victory! Roses fragrance;
Is what imagine the eye.
Little did I know,
Gravely wrong was I.

.

Last day, ate nothing.
Next day, maybe my own blood.
Holy books are daily routines,
While in red dresses the Earth.

.

How short is life?
Thee roll of two dice—
Fate mocked at our face,
No prayers, no cries:
Perhaps funerals? But disgrace.

.

One last bullet, one gun,
With a dreadful hound.
Maybe it wasn't meant to be,
But with all that I have seen,
The Last Bullet is for me...

4. Our Flowers

Far away is the Heaven, beyond every hours
Of the material world of sweets and sours—
The flowers I pluck for you are merely flowers
Grown by God who from His heightless towers
Waters them and drowns the memories of ours
That used to shine but, now in melancholy, it devours
Our days of yore! Our flowers merely— flowers.

.

What did fate bargain and sell in its Store
That we cannot see each other; not anymore?
I stare at the field, sigh our flowers— and nothing more
Feels alive in the land of cruel spring of the poor.
Our sown seeds have risen as flowers of melancholic lore,
But you didn't rise from the grave— you're alive no more—
And Carmela! Dead are the tales of our melodious yore.

.

Every night, I walk past our flowers and kept— hearing
The whispers and tales of demons who kept staring
At the erosion of my heart, which was peering
Through the ribs— the endless pain it was bearing—
The pain of losing you in this world of denying—
Upon this land stretched afar, and was once dying,
But, upon this dead land, now our flowers are dancing.

.

Carmela! You always wanted to hide forever
From this world that claimed our love will never
Be righteous, but little did I know your fever
Would hide you inside Your grave forever;
The grave under the land of our flowers that may forever
Bloom, or may wither in an instance for I can no longer
Bear to see them dance upon the land you sleep forever.

.

Ah! Gone is she. The spirits flew away from the lung,
Let the burial rites be read, the funeral song be sung—
A last anthem for the lover who died so young—
For her, God! Let all the Heavens' bells be rung—
Don't let her fall prey to the evil eye or the sinful tongue—
Bless her from Your Ivory towers,
For our flowers are merely— flowers.

.

Carmela! I know you are not dead,
For upon your grave, the flowers aren't flowers, but instead
Are yourself reborn as flowers with bright and ivory shade—
The petals are those sentences that were left unsaid,
And the vibrant dance upon your deathbed
Are merrily not of demons who sing inside my head,
But of the colorful memories of ours, instead!

.

But, Carmela! Our flowers are merely— flowers.
They'll wither and decay with the passing of every hours,

Like you withered away leaving behind only I of ours—
I try to touch the white petals of your flowers,
But they slide through my fingertips as if the air devours
My fleeting soul who wanders in this field of flowers,
And watches them wave farewell to all that was once ours—
For our flowers are merely— flowers.

.

Ah! Gone I am too. The spirits flew away from the lung,
Let no mortal weep, the funeral song be sung—
A last anthem for the lover who died so young—
For me, God! Let no Hell's bells be rung—
Don't let me die of the broken promises from this tongue—
Bless us from Your Ivory towers,
For our love was merely— a love of eternal hours—
For our flowers are merely— flowers.

5. How Rich The Earth Is

How rich The Earth is for it wraps you
Around her chest with her charms—
How poor I am for I can no longer
Hold you within my arms.

6. The Magpie

From years ago, in the winter moonlight
I sat by the window lattice, darkness had preside—
Hark! The moon rays sing and cry—
For the abyss in my heart left open for demons to pry.

.

Oh, Sophia! I have lost all that is once true—
Sew my soul, and carry me away from the mortals
I implore for there can never be me without you.

.

The tides of winter and nights of December
Had wrought sorrow upon my hopes, I remember—
As the demons reside on my ribs and feast
Upon my love for beloved Sophia who's forever seized.

.

Oh, Sophia! Tell me, what can I do to make you come true?
Tell your God to half-grant my wish to die —
For I must live, for I want to remember you.

.

Ill mortals befriend the nights that had been unkind to me—
For it mocks my days of yore, when happy I used to be.
The poet inside me is dead, for dead is his poetry—
I wish my life had been more than a hymn of insanity!

.

Oh, Sophia! What was it that made you disappear—
Like the death of a beaitiful flower in a garden,
Like the Autumn as the winter arrives, and leaves me in fear?

.

Wicked is the world, wicked is its moon—
For it promises a false verse of meeting you soon.
Sophia, is it you who sings when dusk is past?
Tormenting my soul, this foreign tune— will it ever last?

.

Oh, Sophia, loathe the way you loved me more,
More than I ever could. But then, Death came
Like this song, and took you away from me, forevermore.

.

What is this ruffled song that sings about you?
I ponder— I wonder in hope and in fear too.
Is it a song that mocks my beliefs or mourns for me?
Or another delusion of mine that's never meant to be?

.

Oh, lost Sophia! My room, it is gloomy and so am I—
Foolish I am to think the song, a tantalizing poem—
For it's just the throat of a tuxedo bird from the sky.

.

The moon rays passed the clouds, lending their arms to me,
Carrying me away— a sight no mortal eyes could see!
Then, dared the little shadow to snatch me where I was,
It came swiftly with agony, tears, and a nameless curse—

.

Oh, Sophia! Fluttering into the darkness with an omnipotent cry,
Like a forbidden song, or a tantalizing poem of grief,
All my convictions it began to rob; a black little Magpie.

.

Silently perched the dainty bird above my dark chamber,
Upon the closet that locked portraits of my love, my disaster!
Drifted away from the shore of my dreams and touch,
You still haunt me with the nightmares of such.

.

Oh, Sophia! Have you dressed as this Magpie of Erebus?
To forge our vows of a prophesied eternity
Into a mere unrequited and unfulfilled dream of us?

.

You wanted to choke your neck and shatter my dream—
As I held you tight, my demons famished thy bloodstream.
Sophia, I slaughtered you and thought of killing myself too—
Sophia, I failed for I didn't know my false and true.

.

Oh, beloved Sophia! Now I know and cloudless clear too—
It's not you who flew in as a magpie of our epoch,
It's the devil dressed as a little Corvus of false virtue.

.

Coward and blinded was I, so I couldn't slaughter me;
The knife turned black with blood of Sophia, who loved me!
I carried and laid her underneath the lake beside our house
That we built together with pieces of our love and vows.

.

Oh, Sophia! A forsaken bird of darkness, this Magpie is;
For it wears a drop of devil's blood on its tonigue—
All my memories of yours, my love, it cease.

.

I begged the bird to not haunt me,
But ceasing its singing, it kept staring at me.
Reminding me I killed her on a tainted night like this—
Reminding me I killed my Sophia, whom I dearly miss

.

Oh, Sophia! You'll always remain in my veins and sinew—.
So will the Magpie perch upon my chamber, every year too;
And it will sing a lullaby to me, of my dear you...

7. To Die By Your Hands

Take my heart out of my ribs,
I would die by your hands—
Lurking deep into the abyss,
Inside the walls, I hear voices of my fiends.

.

Take my skin and tear it apart;
For the Angels are dead; demons dethrone
The fleeting flocks played their part;
The petrtified souls sing of home.

.

Take my hands, and trace all the sins
I've done while thou drink my nightmares;
Far I am from forgiveness and redemptions
But, I, finally, am coming home.

8. The Black Box

Horrible! Horrible was the night as I remember
The horrendous gloomy night of October—
That night the world slept and I had no sleep;
As I saw my love in her wet cheeks, she did weep.
My love, she came to me at my bedside
For illness had visited me, she came in like a fair bride.
Dressed all in white— with her saintly fair—
My love she came, and my love did wear.

.

Alas! Alas! The graves hold no tears
For the dead who had surpassed Earthly fears!
Grew darker the night and gone is the moon,
The shadows of the dead will be freed very soon.
My lover will be there too- among the shadows
With her pallid white hands and red, red nose.
She will dance upon the yellow clouds of the night
With her saintly maiden dress of white—

.

Hark! Hark! The echoes below the ground—
What custom makes that dreadful lonely sound?
The floor shook and swooned with the tremors
As the shadows in corners patched the horrors—
Horrors of the past— the past of my Sabine

Who loved me, and sometimes I loved the mortal being.
I love her memories more than I loved her
The hideous tremors below the ground halted never.

.

Slowly! Slowly, I walked down the subterranean chamber
To see my Sabine sleeping with hairs like dark amber—
Her eyes were as black as the deepest abyss,
Her sacred lips were forbidden to every kiss—
Imagined, I, her, in those Heavenly beauties, she would—
But, alas, she sleeps inside the Box of Black wood.
I made the Black Box hide her from any grave,
To keep her away from Decay— Thy Lords protect and save.

.

Hazard! Hazard! The Box had disappeared from its place—
There laid only the dust of the past, and lovers— one less.
I crept deeper into the darkness of the room
With my eyes wide and my heart beating faster—
The black box was visible at the corner, at last—
But the box's nails were torn and opened aghast.
It appeared almost invisible in the darkness—
I kneeled and creaked open the cover with mildness.

.

Alas! Alas! No sooner did I remove the cover,
The white apparelled skeletal arm fell rattling on mine.
And when I thought the terror was finally over,
The corpse grasped my arms and jumped up on my chest,
She wept soundlessly, and broke her rest—

She decayed and breathed her last breath—
Her dark sockets hung on her hideous face—
As she moaned and held my arms with disgrace.

.

"Who? Who is this filthy woman?", I cried and yelled.
"Where is Sabine, my love?", question I held.
The white apparelled skeleton didn't speak a word—
And collapsed there— no moaning was ever heard.
I buried my Sabine, alive and placed her in the Black Box,
But nowhere was she, only this skeleton of whites,
And my lover had gone away from me— for all nights.
Only remains is the Black Box of my bride,
Gone is she, gone is my love, forever from my side.

.

Terrible! Terrible are the human souls,
Once caged, and now free from the bars of bones—
How shall we distinguish the shadows of the grave
From that of the dead who roam in the airy wave?
My love, Sabine came in a form so strange I can't discover,
But her tears from her lonely eyes did drip all over—
She made no sound, no weep, no words she said—
And then I knew, my lover was dead.
And then I knew, my lover was dead.

9. The Valley Of Dead

Beyond the mortal lands,
Death has created a hidden throne,
In a strange valley beyond, and lying alone,
Where the restless living dead
Who were once either human so worst or best
Are now living past their eternal rest.

.

In the Valley of Dead, stretches
The field of lilies that smiles, weeps and waves
Over the unspoiled soil of countless graves.
The forgotten winds and gentle sea
That once tremble across the earthly matter
Now run through the valley's sweet water.

.

Neither any rays of Heaven falls upon the land
Nor fire of Hell burns the valley's sand,
No grave, no tomb can hold the spirits in
That roams in memories beyond once piety and sin.
No mortal belongs to the valley of dead,
For the valley resides in our heart,
For the people who left us, beyond love or hate.

10. Midnight Moth

Stretched against the window panes,
Lies the moth with brown feather—
The rest of the nocturnals sleep while outside, it rains;
Only this moth visits my home in this dark weather.
The wind of the first winter stirs up the trees;
Duller is the daylight than the lamp in my chamber—
The alluring luminesce of the lamp is what the moth sees
Through its red eyes that prey upon the light forever.

.

A long longing for a restful sleep of the eyes
That burn from the exhaustion of daydreaming lies—
Lies that mustn't be spoken and must remain within the soul
Or everything that seems true shall shatter in a whole.

.

The red veins upon the sclera of the eyes tear the white
Into its red patchwork of emotions that were once soluble,
Can no longer dilute into dreams of any wrong or right
Pains that could pass away as quickly as women were able
To leave me like the winter leaves upon spring's demands.

.

The moth, as if, implores to get in so it could rest,
Rather than to disturb the night, to disturb my loneliness—
A stare, more than demonical, upon the moth's eye nests

Inside my thoughts of forgotten days of happiness,
And relieved me from the fear of losing my disparity
With the feelings of missing my freedom, my liberty.

.

Once I too was a king of stretchable lands
Upon which I displayed my own devils— my own tyrants.
On solemn midnight, the arrows rain down on my lands
And the nations I named my own, the nations I fought for,
Turned my empire into grains of dust on my hands.

.

On a single night, died all the spirits I was given
By the God, who on his throne, so late from Heaven
Fell the dews of the defeat of my kingdom and reign—
The victors and traitors locked me away from every plain,
Upon this very rock in the ocean, blindest to every man.

.

I opened the window and let the insect in
And the winged bug flew towards dark walls,
And then to the table and did what I've never seen:
Upon the hot glass covering the fire that crawls,
It kissed the lamp and spread its smeared wings
As if it was the funeral ceremony of its own death.

.

The moth sat there and drank the fire
And succumbed I outgrew a deadly desire—
I realized and I understood it very more,
Some tomb this house is, of whose windows and door

Are mere illusions and I shall never be free anymore.
How delirious it is to think that all my deeds, my sins
Have turned into my own death that laughs within
The very soul of mine, within patches of the moth's wings!

.

I ran up— up towards the attic so dark
To fetch me the chemical that burns. Hark!
The fluttering of the famishing moths lures me
To set my flesh upon the fire, so the spirit may not go free—

.

I drowned my whole robe and soul in kerosene,
Lit my body with the lantern fire that draws the moths in—
The dark crooked house was, once for a life, too bright,
With the flame, I put on as a garment sewed with my sins
And the horde of moths famished upon my flesh set alight
As all I heard was the fluttering of thousand wings
That sings of the Heaven of lies upon which I took birth,
Farewell! Depart I from this very Earth.

RESURRECTION

11. The Visit

Once upon a summer breathe,
There lived a painter at the edge of the city
With whom I had the honor to meet
And when I did meet, I saw a lady so pretty
As a sitter of the painter busy at his duty—
Painting the charming woman of twenty,
Painting silently in his studio, the Athenian beauty.
And when I did stare at his canvas, so rich yet greedy
To be filled with the colors of its master who lived in my city.
Oh, marvelous had he made the painting of beauty,
So vivid, so colorful, so darling in its serenity—
But when I stared at the painter of our city
Little did I know, he was a young boy of no more than twenty.
I asked, "How can you paint so beautifully?
It's not the sitter, but himself a painter paints." he smiled timidly.

.

The next day, I did visit him again
When the city was dull and gloomy,
With the sudden downpour of unromantic rain.
And when I visited him, I saw an old man of eighty,
As a sitter of the painter who seemed crooked but busy
In his painting. Today he sketched with dignity

The man had a countenance of sorrow and tragedy
I looked at the sketch and wondered really—
How talented is the young man who is just twenty!
I asked again, "How can you paint so beautifully?"
"It's not the sitters' emotion but of painters'" He smiled gravely
And alas! He looks so cold and old in his gauntly
Face that had no trace of youth nor any beauty.

.

Again, I visited him after that day,
At night when the lights glowed gaily—
And the moon was pale. I visited him that day.
But nowhere was he who painted so beautifully,
Only was his canvas upon which was a painting glowing dimly,
It was a painting of the night sky with stars glowing vividly.
The painting of stars that seemed to be crying sadly,
Stars that seem to say, "goodbye for eternity."
And thus, once lived a painter in our city.

12. To Art Is To Sin

Heavens have my love in their revered keep,
Forever in the accursed eyes of no sleep—
And those ears hear the echo of Israfil's trumpet,
While lonely sins shine above the deeds' summit—
While thou conjures my dreams, my memories
While thou build my sepulcher of our eternities.

.

Like Azrael, thou come softly, silently in my dreams,
Every night is a stage act of my death, as it seems—
For the slumber of the body who is in sleep so deep
Like worms over my rotting body feast and creep—
And the soul has escaped to thou while the mortal sleep.

.

Thy soul is made up of my dreams on the deathbed
Of lovers' love and my nightmares shade in bloodred.
The sea that drowns my body on the shoreline—
Also flows over the bones of my love, my Caroline.

.

To keep my Caroline alive, I paint her portraits
In one thou smile, one thy fears, and in one, thou cry—
But none justice thy fairness, no amount I left to try!
I burnt all my colors and all my Canvas,
Where I drew thy face of dandelion flowers.

Burnt and kept burning— the portraits lost in hours—
While the wicked truth swallows my lies and devours.

.

My Caroline!
Look at thou! Resurrected
From the blazing Lazarus of thy portrait!
The flame twisted and turned to shape thy body
And Look! thou come back to me, slowly to me.
The entrancing demeanor of thy flame
Wrapped them around my chest,
As if thou came back to me to take what's left to claim,
To make me away with you and all of me that is rest.

.

My Caroline!
I understand now and thou know it too:
Thou came to life, again, with the portraits I drew—
For the order of art is to ensure the survival of our reality,
For the chaos in every art means to deny sanctity.
How indistinguishable is the shadow thou cast
From the shadow of my sepulcher that last
Longer than the living mortal; I—
Whose soul witnesses the Hellfire in front of his eye.

.

Hell has my destiny in its treacherous keep,
Since thou left and I paint thou with no sleep.
And the ears hear the Grand Israfil's trumpet,
While my lonely sins shine above the deeds' summit

Of mine, while thou conjures my truth, my memories—
While I built my destiny where I'll art for eternities.

..

I dared to challenge the Almighty,
For He made thou, the woman of all Beauty,
With His hands but ignorant I
Destroyed His creation
And made myself lie
That I'll resurrect thy liberation
Again, upon this very Earth of every fables,
With my very hands, my very colors—
Even if the saints claim me one of the rebels,
Even if I form myself into a sinner,
Even if my art denies every Prophets' speech,
To keep thou alive, to keep thou with me forever—
I painted thy faces for decades, to keep thou in my reach.

.

But I knew, Caroline, I did
And now I know, I reside in the Hellfire.
I denied our distance, I denied my morality
Where— To Art is to Sin—
To Love is Insanity.

13. The Blood Painter

Winter whispered the tales of terror never told before—
The ghosts of the wind brought the verses of forgotten lore
Of the blood painter, and the tales of his glory and gore
Inside the house of the haunted days of yore—
The House of Livercreek, the painter of a buried lore—

.

The spiders had decorated the Greek walls and Persian floor
With the pale cobwebs that trembled and danced in galore
With the nameless spirits past the House's door—
The spirits of the sitters of the painting of haunted lore—
The paintings of Livercreek- the painter demons adore—

.

Like rain from the Heaven, the lost spirits downpour,
Upon the House of their mortal painter, in galore—
And stayed there, like the ocean waves— cast ashore—
Waited there— for the next tide to reach the shore—
Waited there for the painter who'll return— nevermore!

.

Livercreek had no colors, no turpentine, nor oil in his store—
Nor used he— raw water for the art demons so adore—
Livercreek— the painter upon his mansion of Persian floor,
Explored the art of immortality (it's curse)— and swore
To draw portraits— that will never decay; for evermore!

.

The painter listened to the whispers of his heart's core,
And decided the fate of his art, and their cruel lore—
He would paint his sitters with the blood they bore—
To make the portraits and sitters immortal— for evermore—
Alas! Deals with demons are false oaths and nothing more—

.

The art of Livercreek took the lives and could never restore
The mortals' flesh and sinews of the sitters who wore
Corsets, tuxedos, or silken satins of forgotten lore—
All the dresses were stained with blood that lure
The demons and made the mortals— spirits for evermore.

.

Dwell the spirits inside the painter's House of haunted lore
And sit, and stand in front of their portraits and explore
The geniuses of Livercreek and his works— and implore
To nameless fate to return the painter who swore
To paint paintings with the blood his sitters bore.
As the lore was bestowed, the painter was made sure—
Destroying his art would free the spirits— forevermore.
But in love was he with the art of his cruel gore—
So exiled himself the painter from his haunted lore—
Waited the spirits for his return— returned none— no more.

.

Centuries had passed and the Livercreek house of cruel lore
Still stands tall with its Greek walls and Persian floor—
Only the curtains flutter and nothing more—

The spirits of the blood paintings still roam past the door—
Waiting for Livercreek to return who died long before—
And what remains are the undying art of his cruel lore.

14. Funeral Mutation

The rain made the sky gone caliginous
Like the blackness inside a blind eye—
They: the wind, called spirits of strange universe—
They: the leaves, turned sober, crisped and dry,
Falling upon the drenched land; so mysterious,
That laid between Heavens and Hell where sinners cry.

.

The river made of tears that rolls
Over us, the mortal-forsaken roaming souls,
Whose eyes kept records of the past years,
And unfulfilled buried prophecies of futures—
The souls that rest by the dim Strait of Dover,
Also roam in the lonesome woodlands in November.

.

The North doesn't exist in the world of spirits,
Neither the clock nor time that I mistrust—
Neither exists the pair of wings of spirits that greeds
To fly, but sorrowfully trail over the dust—
For none had cheated death, as equally, it treats,
For to mortals, we're ghouls and haunt we must.

.

The things that lay hidden in this world
Are living and breathing through the eyes of crows—

We fly with our ebony feathers and curled
Every time a lover brings along a rose,
And croaked every time a heart is murdered,
For we're the messengers of death, God did propose.

.

Oh, Sophia! Forgive me for I couldn't keep
The promises that I swore from my very lip—
I had to go for it was Death who called,
For it was a caprice of God, not our fault—
That I died and was killed by drowning myself
Into the lake that was stained with blood of thyself.

.

Oh, Sophia! But I was born again,
When the clouds sang and it began to rain.
I rose from the deep and turned into a crow,
And cried and croaked for you; my love, my sorrow.
Then, the fleeting flocks of the ebony birds
Came and spoke their foreign tongue
That we must visit the mourning graveyards,
For the distant eveningbell has rung.

.

We are the priests of forbidden rituals,
Upon the world of certitude and cruels.
Crows that fly and soar, are like darkness
Upon the sky that cages the humanness
Of walking corpses that breed upon immorality—
And die in graves, crowned by us; our rites, our duty.

.

The Black Corvus sits placidly
Upon the tombstones that recite peacefully
The last verse of the person lying
Underneath the world of darkness and denying.
Among these crows, you can find me too—
Among those people lying beneath the tombstones,
You can dig up and find my bones, too.

15. The Wall

It was on an autumn midnight,
When I sat with the company of your absence,
Listening to the rustling of leaves that had dried,
Inhaling the scent of yours but only its essence—
Lonely and silently, I dreamt a dream that was once true,
About a past that was the only life we knew—
But the past is dead, and love has died,
Time has mocked us, and to us, fate had lied.

.

Memories had succumbed into saintly souls,
That lists our love and only love of ours,
But the souls have been caged by the mortal bones,
So fragile— like on a dried plant blooms two flowers.
"How did you forget me?" I asked,
Staring at the wall of my room, aghast—
"Was it by drinking chemicals of forbidden pharmacy,
Or with a good sleep of a night in serenity?"

.

I stared and stared at the wall, and for hours I did stare—
And pondering, discovered a hole up on it—
A hole no bigger than the pupil of a deer—
And the hole stared at me, the longer I stared at it.
The hole was darker than the devil's tear,

And when I went near it, a mild eerie thud I hear.
A sudden thud! And nothing more was heard—
Fear grew in me— I deemed it to be cursed.

.

Almost swooned but still, I felt a vague urge to invent
The conclusion of the mystery the hole holds—
What horrors (or Pandora's secret) the hole has rent
That it seems to hide some chest of golds—
Or perhaps a skeleton of the ancestor of this house,
Or some vermins feeding upon a dead mouse,
Or maybe a secret kept hidden for centuries,
Or just a mocking vexation of my curiosities?

.

As I kept thinking and thought about the hole
Absurdly grew wider, and wider upon its place
And the inside became visible past the hole—
Almost like a void of black and nothingness.
I dared not to lend my arms but my thought
Whispered back to my body: my hand was brought,
Almost involuntarily, inside the widened hole
To let my arm reach the other side of the damned hole.

.

Procuring callous of my mind, I lent my hand inside
Inside the hole, and no sooner did I,
Then felt a shiver, and my nerves almost died
When another hand clenched lightly upon mine.
Oh, what curse is this that past the hole lives a soul?

Oh, what treacherous game has devised the hole?
Oh, my love! What is the wicked spell your memories had—
Oh, that it created a damned hole on the wall so mad?

.

Ah, what is that hides beyond the hole—
Awakened by memories of my love, who has forgotten me
Perhaps, some invention of my dreams or an actual soul,
Breathing and living past the hole in madness or in glee?
I peered into the hole, now wider than my face
But it was darkness and darkness only inside the place.
Then, I withdrew my hand quickly from the hole,
But the other side seemed to snatch me into the hole!

.

I took an ax and destroyed the wall with the hole,
Aiming straight at the hole, I did strike
And did strike again, until cracks arose from the hole,
And did strike again, and again, until the wall *died.*
With my *good* efforts, the hole is now a door
To the other side of the wall of darkness evermore.
I strode in slowly and silently, no sound I made—
And something stood behind me, my name it said.

.

Behind me walked slowly a slender figure in the darkling,
When I turned to look at the figure,
It was you my love, my dear, my darling who kept lurking
At me— with the beauty and charm so vigor,
It erased the darkness and turned it into a Paradise,

Where my lost love found its home, and did rise,
The saplings of my memories into mellifluous flowers
Which dances to the melody of the love of ours.

.

No sooner did I touch your cheeks,
Everything vanished in the blink of an eye,
And my hand holds apparel so old, and tricks
My consciousness— I found myself caught in a lie:
The old closet was plastered; the wall was raised anew
When I entered the house, and the owners left their Stead—
Leaving behind this damned closet; uncemented.

.

"How did you forget me?" I wept,
But the answer as a secret was kept,
Did you fall in love with our memories as I did,
Or did you fall in love with a mortal instead?
Did you put your love in your prayers as I did,
Or did you bargain our love with the devil instead?
How did you forget me?
How did you forget me?"

16. The Mermaid

I spent my winter days,
In the trials of forgetting you.
Your memories are melting like ice,
And my heart is getting warm, too.

.

You were the ribs that built my chest,
Retreated away like the tidal crest.
I look through my telescope,
For I was vaguely assured of hope
That laid upon the islands far away,
But the clouds yelled and told me to go away—
Through the telescope, and through my eyes,
I could only see the night in its darkest form
That drew the ship named Agatha
Into the wicked tempestuous storm.

.

The gurgling of the briny ocean water,
Started to tear her apart.
Agatha, with the captain, cried louder,
And the nymphs, as spirits, started playing their art.
The moon-blanched nymphs sang solemnly,
About our death, that was destined to be
But suddenly, out of the vortex

That threw the water up to the sky,
Rose up the sea monster in all wrath and vex,
Threw Agatha o'er the cursed sea, where sea serpents lie.

.

Myriad of years, in the sailors' eyes
Vanished away as we lost track of our paradise.
The gold, the rum, and the sugar that was stored,
All lost in the deep, away from every shore,
As it was the only destiny, God bestowed:
The sailors we are, and as sailors, we die,
The deep sirens our funeral song,
The sea our graveyard, and upon corals we lie.
Agatha lost her course, and lost her masts;
The nymphs sang with silent voices
As they kept the sailors' corpses aghast.
The spirits of the ocean drew out Agatha's soul,
From the wooden flesh of tales and rust.

.

The Captain stood still upon the sinking deck,
Looking at his Agatha as winds made his beard shake.
Agatha looked at him and smiled goodbye,
The old man smiled with tears in his eye—
He loved her like darkness is to be loved;
In secrets between the shadows and blackness—
Agatha held him tight and parted away from us,
Both sank into the ocean deep and darkness.

.

The Seagulls laughed at us and mocked
Our imprisonment upon the ocean,
As they flew past the wooden skeleton of Agatha,
And the Mediterranean winds welcomed the rain.

.

Oh, Serena!
Away I am, away from you—
The memories of us reflected upon
My eyes, upon every wave of the ocean, too.

.

Oh, Serena!
I spent my winters, forgetting you—
But I couldn't do it, because
You reside in my dreams, and in all that is true.

.

Oh, Serena!
Drowning I am, drowning in the ocean blue—
Wish I could see you one last time because
Drowning feels like going home, but there won't be you.

.

The sea serpents crawled up and wrapped their skin
Over my legs, over my waist, and pulled me in,
Into the deep of the ocean heart, where no light can reach—
The briny water of cursed sailors choked my neck
As I inhaled the poisonous elixir into my arteries,
Then cried the lonely clouds that made the heavens shake,
The sea drew me within the land laid hidden for centuries—

The land of deep, sculpted with seabed and coral bones,
And awaited a strange creature upon the stones.

.

The creature swam towards me,
Placidly, and slowly to me—
My name, it asked and whispered to me,
But the water shut my lips and I couldn't answer,
Then it came closer, and it was clearly visible—
It had the torso of a maiden of prelapsarian glow,
And the rest was made of what makes fishes flow.
She was the mermaid of the deeps,
But when I looked at her face
It had the trace of Serena, her eyes, her lips,
For Serena, it was, in all her beauty and grace.

.

Oh, Serena!
Is this really you,
Or is it death telling tales of you?
Is it really you, whom my loved?
I pondered, as my body became numb,
I asked her but silently she laughed
With her eyes, while her lips stayed dumb—
"Is it you, my Serena, whom I loved,
My Serena, my love?" I asked.

.

The mermaid held my hands,
Grasping my mortal body

And haunting my inner spirits—
Gently, she dragged me deeper,
Deeper into the ocean abyss,
Where no light reached.
I looked up and all I could see
Was the shimmering moon in glee.

.

Oh, Serena!
I loved our love, always I will love you—
Even though my fate designed my destiny
Into the deep seabed, to drown without you—
I wish I could tell you my tales of missing you,
For I wanted to love you for infinity,
But as a liar, I die,
As a sinner, I rest,
For eternity.

17. The Chair Of Lazarus

Ah! The night fell and broken is the oath
That kept the darkness of hauntings, away—
The oath that, with no knowledge,
Was given to mother who passed away
Upon such malice night that surpassed a cruel day,
When the moon painted the cities, upon Earth, who lay—
I stood in front of the vault door; almost motionless.
As broken is the oath and no statements to confess—
Open is the vault, and the chair turned restless.

.

The chair in the vault of our crooked house
Is hungry again, for it breathes and lives
Waiting for its prey as broken are the vows
I kept with mother who passed away
Leaving me and this chair alone, upon the world of decay—

.

Born was I; deceased and dead
With no beating heart— mother said.
But gifted was she with this chair of woods so red—
The chair that could give life to the silenced and dead.

.

Neither Heaven-made nor sculpted in the Hell
The chair seemed a possessed entity in the cell

Of this Villa owned by a doctor who gifted the chair
To my mother who died as its last heir.

.

Mother said, "The Chair of Lazarus is accursed
By the doctor who failed to save his wife
And built this seat of magic and cursed
No matter the wound, or cut by a knife
Once placed the corpse on the furniture
It'll be reborn again no matter the bruises,
The injuries, the pain, or the fracture.

.

And born was I; a womb already dead
Mother placed my body on the seat
With doubts and the mourning of tears she shed.
Cried I; a newborn son with childish heat
In this very home, this very vault— death faced defeat.

.

Still, never I thought the tales to be true
For I was a man with doubts in magics, too—
So one midnight, I walked down the street
And found a white cat who saw me and retreat
But clever I fed it and filled with a love so deceit
Brought it home, and killed it with scissors
And scattered the blood that stained all the mirrors
That reflected my insanity and my terrors.

.

Placed the hideous beast upon the chair of rebirth

And waited I for hours but my patience— time devoured.
And never returned the animal upon the Earth.
Scared I with rage but recollected my intuition—
That no animal but only human are subjects of resurrection,
But how a chair could distinguish an animal iwth men
When we ourselves cannot even if we are the most sane.

.

On the next night, I implored the landlady
Of the neighboring house to help me with the house duty.
Kind lady came in and picked a glance at the chair,
And in terror, before her fears she could share—
I stabbed right into her chest and pierced her heart,
Convulsed she, and convulsed only once
Before I, placed her on the chair upon the very Earth.
But hours passed and she never returned,
The old lady died, and my rage into curiosity it turned.

.

Later, I invited my lover, Marie
For the last supper of her life—
She drank the wine and kissed my lip,
As gently I stabbed her with a knife,
And broke the promises of love I never meant to keep.
Beside the stairs, I took her to the cell,
Where reside the chair that belonged to no Heaven, or Hell!

.

Maybe, the Landlady was at such an age,
That the oldness of her already welcomed death

And thus the chair cared no more—
And thus the chair rejected her rebirth, for evermore!
So, the virtue of the chair was greatly hidden
Deep in the young blood like that of the maiden
Who loved me true, and sometimes I loved her too.

.

The corpse of Marie sat still as a calm river
Hours passed and she didn't return, never—
Marie was gone from the mortal land, forever!
And lonely I, with the chair, glanced at her body with terror,
Decided to bury all the three in some grave near
But the outside world might witness my insanity, I fear.
So, clever I: wrapped the bodies in a whole
And placed them under the floor by digging a giant hole,
Under the chair and plastered the floor, again
I laughed timidly, even if the chair bore no gain.

.

I broke the vow I kept to mother:
"The vault door will not be opened, forever!"
But here I am, sealing the door;
Shutting the chair of mythomaniac lore,
Trapped within the vault of a dark history; for evermore.

,

Weeks passed since I glanced at the chair
I killed a cat, the old lady, and Marie— I couldn't dare
To believe I did and reconcile with my morality;
Am I really some Caliban, or some demon entity?

At the midnight when the red moon hangs in the sky,
I trotted towards the vault door with fear, and pry
Upon the mysteries of the world inside the small room,
And the darkness of the creaking chair lurked with hunger,
Aghast with malignance, I closed the door of the chamber.

.

I ran upstairs in fear, but suddenly groaned a cat, I hear.
Groaned again, from the chair vault, as if it would tear
The house apart and all I did was to stare,
Silently back at the vault door that trapped the chair
From up the stairs; rattling myself in fear
As the cat groaned louder— I could hear.

.

Locked me in my room, with despair
But suddenly, a laugh in broken cheeks— I could hear.
Laughed again, with pauses and demonical— I grew a fear.
It was the laugh of the landlady who sat on the chair
And returned again, so she could tear
My solidarity apart and all I did was stare
Silently at the darkness of my eyelids, shut in fear.
As distinct her voice became— I could hear.

.

Then, slowly and with crooked steps, on the wooden stair
Walked someone up towards my room, I couldn't dare
To recollect my senses, and towards the door, I stare—
Weary and fearing with nameless terror,
A knock on my door, a sharp attack in my heart,

Marie called my name, the door remained the guard.
She slammed the door with her bare hands,
And slipped away from my feet, the psychic lands.

.

But would that mean they all were resurrected?
Or is it just the images inside my head?
That could no longer distinguish what's reality and a dream
For, they are reborn again, as they seem.

.

I opened the door;
With some hypocritical valor—
But found none, only the terrifying lore
Of my last weeks of horrifying yore.
For the vows mother gave; I tore.
The same happened every day, reminding me of my gore:
Groaned the cat, the lady's laugh, and knock on my door—
With Marie, my love calling my name from behind the door—
But when I opened it, there was the chair and nothing more.

.

In the month of November,
I decided to kill myself for I could no longer
Bear the hauntings of the house!
For, since the day, I broke the vows,
Since I killed the beings with no remorse, nor shame
How many days passed on Earth, and how months came?
Many raging hearts who seeked answers, I couldn't tame,

But broken was the oath: Marie calls my name.

.

I slit my throat and blood stained my hands,
And at the vault downstairs the chair stands—
Waiting for me to come out of my chamber,
So it could witness the life it gave me, passed away.
I groaned and struggled with the open neck;
As my hands shivered, and my body shook,
As I held the blood to stop flowing from my neck—
The chair watched, the Life it gave and now away it took.

.

But I went towards the chair,
To protect me from dying here—
The lives I took, their return I could hear
And I will return too; with no despair.
I sat on the chair and waited for my rebirth—
But my veins stopped and stopped spinning the Earth.
And my heart stopped beating— no more!
And silence fell upon the house, forevermore...

18. The Weeping Statue

The mortal has been silent
And succumbed in the solitude,
Amidst these dark thoughts
That grasp my soul—
The statue of Paulina,
There with a timid smile, it stood
At the corner of
The forsaken caliginous dining room.

.

The entrancing art
Of thy eyes has tarnished,
By the breath of God,
Or by the gaze of Demons—
Thou hold, hopelessly,
A petrified rose,
Whose freshness vanished,
By the clock that ticks
Every midnight
When thou come to my side.

.

For lovers and love are etched
Upon the gates of eternity,
Thou and I live past

All beyonds and infinity.
For thou are of spirit made,
Even if Angels renounce you a "mystery"
Thou shall forever be mine,
For I paint my dreams with thee.

.

Thy apparels are as pale as
Thy hands and my dreams—
Though thou stand in the corner
Of darkness and misery that screams
My name. You still shine
As lucid as you used to be,
When you talked more words
And swayed with me, and loved me.

.

The caprices of fate stole
My love, my Paulina from my touch
I wanted her to be my "forever"—
And nothing much.
I gambled all my futures
And pasts upon this sole belief
That my Paulina will return,
As she, and her love for me, live.

.

To me, my silence and sorrow seem
As a nightmare, or a fever dream
Which is contagious to the bones

That cling to thee forever.
Upon the drowsy mountains of June,
Lies the bewitching sinister moon
That lures the broken poets near,
But I stood and stand with my heart, here.

.

Oh, Paulina of my truths! Where thou art?
Where have thou gone like verses of Mozart?
Thy lover; I wait for you here and now—
I implore, come back to me one last time
For all of mine is breaking, and so is our vow.

.

I look at my love, my Paulina
And she kisses me with her white placid lips,
And holds me with her cold tender hands
While the moon rays clash with armies
Of fate. The stars have gone sober
For 'tis the dark wicked night of December.

.

I try to breathe and every time I do,
I smell the saintly scent of yours.
I try to search and every time I do,
I could only see this effigy of yours.
I despise the statue for being my Paulina,
I beg my eyes for this isn't her—
For my beloved is gone forever—
For I took her life and placed it inside

The stones and my love in the statue reside.

.

The Angels have declared me a sinner, too—
For I challenge God and his might of creations,
For I am an artist— for I sculpted the statue.
But in front of our love, all the Heavens bow
For we loved more than love itself
For you are forever with me, here and now.

.

Oh, Paulina! Tell me how you still smile
When there's nothing in the world to beguile.
How can you still hold onto that rose
When it's gone and nothing's left but its ghosts.
Oh, Paulina! Tell me, do thou still love me?
Or are you just standing and waiting
For my erosion— my death to come to me?
Is it really you in this whiteness, my loving?

.

Memories glimmered in the soul,
As I kept staring at the statue, alone—
My Paulina was a lady of ethereal beauty—
A Maiden who belonged to no dream, or city,
But who belonged only, and only to me.
The ghouls of midnight breeze
Rushed in from the broken window lattice
And remind me of everything, Of I and thee.

.

Decades ago, I sat with my Paulina by the moonlight
And kissed, gently, her cheeks that felt so bright.
She and I promised our "forever"
By carving our oaths on the stars
With the same knife, I used to protect her
From the insanity of this world, and its sorrow.
I did not want to slaughter my beloved, never!
I wanted her to be written
Upon the parchment of my forever,
Because it is I, who truly love and adore her.

.

I look at my Paulina's fingertips and delude myself
With the dream of their warm touch, of thyself—
I hold my Paulina and realize;
Her body is as cold as the petrifying eyes
Of Medusa and the Greek tales of lament and lies.

.

'Tis not my Paulina, for my Paulina is dead—
"I will see you again, my love", she said,
When I was drowning in her blood,
When she implored me as her beloved
To take her life away, for she knew
She'll always be the paragon of my virtue.

.

I understand now, and very clear too
My Paulina died long ago, and it's just a statue
Who haunted me on every forbidden night

And wrought vague hopes upon my sight—
But my love has drowned in the abyss,
When I bid her goodbye with a farewell kiss,
When her blood summoned all my Demons
And snatched her into the forsaken Elysium.

.

I turned my back away from the effigy
And walked to the window, tracing my tragedy.
I shut windows and doors of the chamber
I look back at the statue, it still smiles, like her—
I hold the cold stone one last moment
And stared at her empty white eyes
As it reflected my inner torment.
Then I choked the hard neck of the idol,
Holding her whole structure and shape
And demolished her whole body,
Before her soul, and my love could escape.
I shattered my Paulina and let myself live,
For I had always been the monster,
For I thought my Paulina was my forever.

.

Oh, Paulina! I turned away
And walked along with my insanity,
Breathing the memories of ours
But when I looked back at the broken statue—
The beheaded eyes started to cry
As blood ran through her cheeks, and there they dry.

19. Hands Of A Poet

The leaves of the crooked tree shake,
Along the waves of the dark forest lake,
By the winds of a forgotten tale—
When lived a poet of unknown name,
Upon this very land and at the bank of this lake
Whose writings can make the very Heavens shake.

.

He once had a wife whom he loved dearly
But alas, a liver disease killed her early
Than normal death— and the poet grew a sudden hate
For the sanity of the world and the caprices of his fate,
And he, in sorrow, himself tried to kill him early—
But the spirits of his unwritten poems held him dearly.

.

And thus, at the bank of this very lake, resided the poet
Inside the small cottage of his love and hate.
He lived, and lived on for years with his fear—
Deep in his heart, a grave sorrow he did bear—
But as time passed, his poems too bore his hate
For this world, and his life as a broken poet.

.

As an admirer of his works, I venture to the forest
Deep into the barren trees where he had his house rest.

In the darkness of evening, I reached the cottage
Upon whose brick walls had grown viridian sage.
Only the skeleton of the house is all that was rest,
Left alone and isolated in the shadowy forest.

.

I knocked at the door— no response I did gain,
As I stood there motionless, and knocked once again.
After minutes, the door creaked open, and stood a figure
At the shadows of the interior with darkness so vigor.
"Who are you?" the man asked, and he did ask again,
"Who are you?" No sorrow in his voice I did gain.

.

I told him who I was, and he told me he was the poet,
The same poet who lost his wife— the poet named Goethe.
He didn't lend his hand for a greeting,
And allowed me inside his cottage without hesitating.
"I am sorry for your loss", said I to Goethe
"What loss? What they say is rubbish!" said the poet.

.

At first, I couldn't understand what he said
But when I saw his wife standing behind the door shade.
I was horrified and asked, "Who is she?"
"My wife, my beloved Sephalia", smiled the man in glee.
The pale woman walked silently past the door shade,
"My beloved is alive." Goethe smiled and said.

.

I asked him, "Why don't you write poems anymore?"

But he spoke no words as if there was some dark lore
Behind his life as an artist of words, love, and poetry—
As if he had some secrets kept in dark for eternity.
Eternity within his poems of some mysterious lore
That seemed nothing to be mourning for— anymore.

.

The pallid lady moved silently back the door,
Busy in her household chores and perhaps, nothing more.
But she did glance at us in intervals, and in silence
With her morbid eyes like pearls of forbidden oceans—
"Is something wrong, sir?" asked the poet, and nothing more
When I asked, "Sephalia's dead, then who's behind the door?"

.

"False! False! Hark, Sephalia! He, too, thinks you are dead,
What false and mere mortal statements the world had said
About you! You are alive here in front of me
And yet, the world claims you are gone for eternity."
With his hoarse voice, Goethe stood and nothing more he said
With a ravenous look in his eyes like those of the dead.

.

He threw his arms and yelled at me,
"How dare you say she is dead and gone from me?"
But when he threw his arms, something peculiar I did notice
He had no hands; his arms ended at his wrists.
I did tremor as he yelled, "Look at my hands, look at me!
I bargained my hands for my love to stay with me."

.

I asked solemnly, "Why did you do that to yourself?"
Because I love her more than the poetry of myself—
I love her more than my poems, more than anything else
Why she must die? Leaving me with my poems, nothing else?
She is the muse of my art! How I can write alone myself
About love, about joy? Tell me, tell me yourself!"

.

The poet crumbled in sorrow and mourned
"Can you see her standing there? Perfect as those stoned
Greek Goddesses. I wrote poems with her corpse's blood
To return her to the world from the graveyard
She did return with all her beauty, but I was stoned
To see my hands eroded from my fingertips as I mourned."

.

Goethe sat on his cruel chair and looked at his hands,
As if memories in his brain had to run some errands—
"The more I write with her blood, more did vanish my finger
My palms eroded from where they used to linger.
The poem was finished and completed was my errands—
In my sleep, Sephalia returned but not my hands."

.

He paused and started laughing loud and yelled
"She came! She came back to me and I held
Her Rosy red cheeks with my wrists' end
She smiled softly, eternal pleasure was gained
When she kissed my forehead with her lips and held

My wrists with her hands." "She's alive!" he yelled.

.

Goethe jumped from his chair and the lady stood there,
The poet swayed like a madman and I did stare—
I knew something was wrong and ran to the door,
And decided not to stay inside the house— not anymore.
The maniac laughed endlessly as the lady did stare
At me, from the window of the house that stood there.

.

It had been a decade since I visited the poet
But still haunts my spines: the memory of Goethe.
As the readers of this poem may seem—
I remember distinctly, it wasn't any dream.
At the end of the forest, still resides the house of Goethe,
Who loved his wife dearly, and once was a good poet.

20. The Scientist

Emmett:
"Winds that blow over the desert of treason
Found me sick for sickness of the heart
Is to be found within the flesh for no reason—
For reasons are abstract thoughts that measure
No less than the mind which holds no treasure.
But you shall know; from 'abstract' rises the idea
And then, to scientific practice; my Veronica."

.

Veronica:
"My love, do you still believe that your science
Can stop the deathbell that sings our goodbyes-
The deathbell inside our wicked souls that chimes?"

.

Emmett:
"Do not doubt- do not feel weary of my morals;
Veronica, I know you shall die soon but feel no horrors-
For even in death- all is not lost for it's shown
That it's in memories- everything is lost and turns stone.
But my memories and my life are bound within you,
Trust me, you shall reborn be again, upon this Earth, anew!"

.

.

Veronica:
"Upon this deathbed of mine, I lie
Love, tell me you'll return to me for my heart
No longer beats- no more- no tears I can cry."

.

Emmett:
"Veronica, my beloved! Breathe, breathe for me-
Are you dead or playing an act in the night
The night that itself sleeps- only awake is the soul in me
And- truly dead you are- as I hold you tight.
But no grave, no cremation can hold you away from my touch
For the Scientist I am and I'll bring you alive
And to your life very much."

.

In grief of heart and more in curiosity of conscience,
Emmett held the dead lady around his chest-
Sobbing in pain and observed for his science-
He took his Veronica to a place divorced from the rest.
Round the crooked stairs, beneath the wrecked floor,
The lover took her to the chamber of his experiments,
Dressed with the skull and bones of cruel lore
Of the scientist who experimented to cage the souls
Of the humans who lay 'round the chamber as bones.

.

Round the seven pillars that held the ceiling tight,
Emmett placed Veronica at the center on that very night-
Laid her corpse on the bed and strapped her tight,

And closed the door and shut the chamber light.
Emmett placed the body and watched it through the glass
The scene of Veronica sleeping still and quiet. Alas!
Turned on the levers and gears howling like hyena
Emmett watched closely the corpse of his Veronica.

.

Emmett:
"Love! I witnessed your body descend and now watch it rise;
My invention proving true in front of my eyes.
I killed all these men and women just for this day
Where I will not let you die and fade away.
Fragile vase this body of yours is- water is the soul,
I'll not let it flow away and I'll love again,
I will fall in love again with you in this new 'whole'.
Yes! Murderer, I am and even if it's so-
For the sake of my science, I sacrificed these bodies in a row,
For the trials of my experiment that never succeeded
Is now a reality- from the corpse rises the soul that preceded
Death and now surpasses it too-
Watch my lover rise with all her glow, her virtue!"

.

Veronica:
"Devils demand dear's death-
In love: memories live-
In memories: love decay-
Decay the whole in death;
Too late, too late..."

.

Emmett:

"Love! My Veronica! Witness your rebirth-
My beloved! You've returned upon this very Earth.
Hark! Here I am! Waiting for you-
Return to me; my science has returned you.
Oh, Veronica! Look at me with your eyes again,
Look into my eyes, where only your memories reign."

.

Veronica:

"Raise no barriers for cracked open is the vase
Towards home the gentle water flows-
The river returns to the eternal ocean;
Away it goes, away it goes..."

.

Emmett:

"Halt! Love! Where are you flying away?
Here I am, your lover- please, don't go away.
Wait and don't go. How can you leave your lover so-
And be silent like distant stars. Please, don't go."

.

The lady died and her pure fleeting soul
Left the scientist in the chamber alone.
Tried the scientist to again fall in love with her
So he tried to capture the soul and cage it forever.
But purity such as souls don't live where evils breathe-
To the Holy- they return; to God- they retreat.

The life God gifts, the mortals had poisoned it-
Like the lonely scientist drinks his demise
Inside the dark chamber with his deceit.

REDEMPTION

21. What Memory Holds

If we could ever learn to trap our souls,
Might we learn what memory holds?
If we knew what our bones turn into,
Might we learn this life's a dream too?

22. A Hypocite's Poem

Contagious solace of a vague light
Contained secret for a thousand decades—
Sanddust; kept hidden from commoners‘ sight—
Little by little, the shield crumbles and fades.
Bewitching air and brave men's hold,
Everyone smiles while the hypocrite cries.
For the hypocrite has a story to unfold,
For time untold, his life implores to summarise.

.

Echoed through the walls; childhood uncertainty
Etched upon each window—pondering life.
So fragile, worthless yet hopeful entity
He is— Like the blade of a Sisyphian knife;
Blunt and dull. Of high virtue, higher conceit
Yet so trivial and much of a weakling,
Horrors of life wait for him; he knew a bit.
Humor the hypocrite— for he finds life entertaining!

.

Soldier on! hypocrite, now a Hoplite of secret lore;
Shouldering duties you have never dared—
For his life isn't his life anymore.
Now, comes forth the time which he feared.
The hypocrite, now, has a heart; he must be a lover—

For he is now a poet, he knows how to love.
Of his lover's dreams, he's a nameless wanderer,
Of the life of that lover: two ghosts to belove.

.

It has been decades since he's a careless fledgling—
It is now arduous for him not to doubt his morals—
For others have forsaken him and his life of denying,
The hypocrite feels like the stranded seabed of corals.
Like the Kings of Sophocles: tragedy awaits for him too;
The thrill that rushes with every smoke he burns
He thinks he dies a little every day— False or true
He despises him too, as death with dignity he yearns.

.

Solitude of the evening star, the hypocrite sighs,
Solemn Selene sings with lyres of dreams,
The hypocrite is old now and, perhaps wise—
As the sight in his eyes shimmers and dims,
The wrinkles time made upon his face,
Mocks the many lives he left behind—
But that's not an elegy that is a disgrace
Because he'd embrace the end, the memories remind.

.

No lovers, no mourners' hugging the hypocrite
More tightly, yet gently than the alienated earth is.
Now the hypocrite too, cloudless clear, knows it:
He was more than a vessel of exile and memories.
For all of his life, he longed for death and demise—

For now, below the Earth, as dust he lies,
He wants to live like the tales of Hesiod's tune—
Yet he hopes to meet his Craftsman soon.

23. Villains

If we were born villains,
Would we show mercy to the tyrants?
Or become villains in their epics?
A gamble of God, this world is—
He knows we are more insane
Than the Devil is,
More pure than the angels are;
Heaven And Hell belongs to sinners of here and afar.

.

If we were born villains,
Were we allowed to fall in love?
Or shackled by self-loathing and darkness?
Love is violence, they say
For the Lords claim to love us
But they slaughter us too, every day.
Not they feel heartless and wrong?
They feel powerful and perhaps strong.

.

If we were born villains,
Would we become harbingers of death?
Or Pagan of a world so false and delusional?
If so, the heroes and saviors would be
Those who were born villains like us

But found out there's no construction of morality—
Those who are free and forever free
From the boundaries of life and its vanity.

24. When

When the moon is gone
And the stars don't shine,
When the night is cold
And the tides don't rise,
When the dawn is a distant memory,
When the doubts sing in you like a symphony
And you still don't hate yourself and wait,
And wait patiently;

.

When you know
Your dreams are shattering
Yet you're still fixing its piece,
When your existence
Is questioned and you're pondering
Yet you are still writing your story in peace,
When you think you've won,
And life chooses to fail you again,
When you thought you were losing
And still forcing your heart to pump,
Yet not afraid to start from the beginning;

.

When all the Kings and crowds named you a misery,
And when you hear your truths coated with lies

Of enemies, yet not falling into their traps of treachery,
When all men and women start acting nice
To you, yet you do not give away your heart fully,
When you've sinned and repented for it
Immediately, and return back to what's Holy.

.

When the dawn isn't here
But you're still standing with the lantern,
Waiting for every second of every minute
And yet, naming them your own,
When the all of yours had to erode
And yet you're still holding on,
With your faith, hope, and actions
Sewed towards one destiny;
Then you'll realize,
You are all at the top of the mountains, all alone,
But you are finally
The Man, the universe designed you to be.

25. Thy

Thy companions are foes,
Thy races waging war,
Thy *religion* has diminished—
Thy and thy world's end is near.

26. When God Cried

Wisdom sleeps tonight—
Death sits placidly on Her hidden throne
On the valley sightless of mortal sight—
The nameless valley of the dead lying alone.
The cold winds blow over the land
Where also blows the wandering pride
Of men, now grains of sand,
Who were once dancing below the mortal light!

.

Love cried tonight—
Death has fallen ill, and *Sickness* has taken Her,
Lying Her upon the valley's grass tonight—
Upon graves of men who once denied Her.
She cried, "Even the Prophets had to die,
Why do you sin? Why do you lie
Upon the material Earth, who can't revive
The guests of mine who thrived to survive?"

.

Death mourns tonight,
"He is The One who loved me, gifted me this land
And named me the Queen—
He who gifted you your soul and body of sand—
Why did you name him tyrant tonight

When you're the man who sins?"

.

Death died tonight—
God loved her and told her to escort
The fleeting souls to the Grand celestial court!
And God for the first time cried and wept
For the Lover who fulfilled the promise she kept.

.

The world sleeps tonight—
Moon held witness to the liars,
Who promised at day and broke it at night.
Sun held witness to the deniers,
Who denied pity and embraced pride.
Stars held witness to the sinners,
Who had sin and never returned to the Right.

.

Death died tonight—
With tears in Her eyes that drowns the universe,
And God cried for the first time
For if the world was sick, Death was the nurse.

.

Death died tonight—
Wisdom and *Love* sings Her funeral song
Yet, the world *peacefully* sleeps tonight.

.

Death died tonight.

27. Fools And Intellects

Fools are foolish,
Intellects have their knowledge—
Both of them wish to be
The other upon the world's stage.

28. The Sparrow That Flew Away

Yesterday, the sparrow perched upon the peach tree,
Singing and praying for today to come—
Today did come, and the sparrow
Spans its wings in joy and flies away.

.

Today, the sparrow that flew away,
May never return tomorrow,
Or, tomorrow may never come—
And thus, the sparrow soars high today.

29. Death Greets Life

Life/ Death:
"May The Almighty forgive
The way I am tangled with thee,
For I am the opposite of what thou are,
I cannot see the reflection of thine in me."

.

Death/ Life:
"Fellows think I am older than time,
But full of sorrow and sleep.
I envy the soft gaze of thy stare,
And thy wide shadow lurking deep."

.

Life/ Death:
"With love, either wrong or true,
How many cherished thou and thy grace
But the pilgrimage thou pay to every soul,
All those truths behind thou bring disgrace."

.

Death/ Life:
"The shimmering twilight is a reminder,
Of how eyes are closed for eternal slumber—
Of how thou and the mortal cease to be
A fickle memory, better not to remember—"

.

Life/ Death:
"When I stare at the grave of stars,
The sky would no longer be blue.
The clouds of a sobbing sky
Are just chariots of demons in my view."

.

Death/ Life:
"For I'm already born before thou start to breathe,
We both are intertwined in thee,
One's time passes, one's get closer,
For I would wait centuries for thou to come to me."

30. Blind Eyes

How lovely madness is—
The madness that sacrifices a lover's dream
And transforms the lover into a poet.
How beautifully he writes
The tales and rhymes of his fictional lies
That painfully meets
With the *Blind* eyes.

.

How deadly a disease love is—
That contaminates every sane
And turns them into poets— into stories.
How beautiful it is to see—
Love can be rendered
Into poems with loveless memory
That tries to erode but painfully meets
With the *Blind* eyes.

.

How envious the dark ocean is—
For many poets have learned its rare language—
The poets who dream to drown
Along the same gurgling voices of the sea.
How tragic, yet silent, is one's demise
That peacefully meets

With the *Blind* Eyes.

LOVE

31. If Love Could Bleed

If Love could bleed,
It would sing about you—
If memories could bleed,
It would mourn for you—
If tragedy could bleed,
It would be me and you—
If love could bleed,
It would loathe me too.

32. Love is Worship

For love is to worship,
And to worship is to pray—
I pray that my memories of you
Shall never die, nor decay.

33. Below The Earth

Below The Earth
You rest,
And I am poor.
I have nothing,
Nothing to offer you
Than my tears.

.

Above the stars
You reside
And I am hopeless.
I still sit
With your shadow
Whom you feared.

34. Goldfinch

The nothingness in my mind
Devours my soul like a dead butterfly,
Trying to flap its wings,
Shattered by the gust of gaily strong wind.

.

Every breath I take feels like the first of snow;
Mild yet corrosive.
Everywhere I look feels like the July rain,
Melancholic and destructive.

.

I would stare at myself,
My reflection on the water would smile.
My body would descend to the depth of the lake,
I would gaze at the dampened sunrays.

.

The specter wind comes gushing in,
Blowing all over the unkempt corners
In my room that shrinks every second.
A goldfinch would whistle on my windowpane,
While taking its last breathe
Before it flies away—
It would remind me of mother.

.

Mother was enchanting—
She would wear a black gown at midnight,
Walking alone on the corridor singing lullaby.
And when the morning came in silently,
She would disappear placcidly.

.

At the depth of the lake,
The voice of mother can be listened,
"Come too close to me, you suffocate—
Go too far from me, away you fade."
And yet, there existed the faint whistle
Of the soaring goldfinch that flew away.

35. The Song Of Your Ribs

A distant song sung by your ribs,
Winds that shake the delicate trees
Sings about the buried heart of mine,
Or left bare in the deep ocean abyss.

36. Lost Memory

Last night, your lost memory visited my heart,
As spring visit the wilderness, placidly,
As breeze visits slowly in deserts of treason,
As a sick person is found ill without any reason.

.

Last night, your memories visited my heart,
As winter recedes from the wilderness, slowly,
As the breeze echoes the silence of your footsteps,
As peace slowly and silently descends on one's sickness,
As Death placidly smiles— and the ill must smile back.

37. Rebels

A land of sands and bones,
A dream as trivial as time;
The Rebels are born there.
Rebels, they hallucinate
A faraway place
As old as the ocean tides.

.

A wretched city of flags and flights,
There's not a single country flag in sight—
Except they hurdle up in the dust,
Yet, all my rebels die for it every day—
Rebels, they *too* have stories to say.

.

A sky made of ghosts and city smokes,
All my rebels howl to the stars.
They kneel to none but truth—
Rebels, they have learned to hide their scars.

.

An ocean made of tears and blood,
All my rebels swim across the shallows.
They dive deeper into the blind water—
Rebels, they are all destined to gallows.

.

A fire lit by an unknown dogma,
All my rebels burn themselves to its flame—
They scream as they turn to ashes—
Rebels, they all have lost their name.

.

Rebels, they wear their lovers' parchment
On the rotten corpses of their soul—
Rebels, they have a nation to save—
Rebels, they have their blood outsold.

.

A death made of ecstasy and glory,
All the ghosts of my rebels wander alone.
Yet, soldier on my Rebels!
We have a paradise yet to be built—
And a long road yet to walk—
Either together, or *maybe* alone.

38. Youth

When I was young
And I didn't know
There's so much in the universe
So much above this Earth.

.

I was young, and I dreamt
Of being old, wise, and a human.

.

I am old now,
And perhaps wiser—
I belong to this Earth,
And to this earth, I shall return.

.

I am older, and I dream
Of being young, reckless, and a human.

39. Mother Of All Poets

Love! The mother of all poets and art!
Who shall love you when they know well,
You are the devil who broke their heart?
And upon your altar, one must put the nail
To sacrifice your soul for the sake of merriness
Because you are the one who took it away
From the lover and left him in grey and loneliness
As he writhes in pain, in grief, and in hope each day.
But as days passed, the lover grew wise,
Leaving behind his wandering in the epoch of past
To seek for you as if a treasure hidden in the skies,
As he realized, it's love that had to last,
Not the lover who promised an endless forever—
No matter what form it takes- love decays never.

40. About You

I wish I could write the way I dream;
insanity.
I wish I could write more about you;
tragedy.

NOTES

I

Human intelligence has its deep roots in human insanity, or better to say: human insanity has its deep roots in human intelligence. To the stagnant world, insanity is anything that causes the ripple that may disappear or turn into waves. The metaphysical world is unexplored properly, not because of its non-physical nature but rather because it's a very dynamic state- it moves and is in constant motion. The stagnant world can barely get a hold of it. Likewise, insanity is one of the pillars that hold this metaphysical world.

Every artist is an insane being, and every insane person is either an artist or once was an artist. Also, keep in mind that by the term "artists" I am not in any way referring to the painters or the poets. I am referring to each one of those souls who dare to venture beyond morals.

Once you deny the moralities, you are honored with the title "*insane.*" You have successfully caused a *ripple in the stagnant system.* Now, you must *invent* a new morality because you have proved the old morals wrong. And as I said earlier, you must invent (or create) a new morality or set of moralities than to discover them. *To discover it implies that it existed in the past and still exists in the present*, and as it exists, it means you have not yet freed yourself from the shackles of old moralities.

Thus, to create "art" is to create new sets of moralities.

II

Often, when the man faces the morbidity of his brain in physical form, he dreams. When he starts to dream, the imagination becomes so artistically vivid, like Botticelli or Raphael, that he understands what he paints with his dreams can never be painted in complete senses or in a waking state. And often, such dreams linger for so long, exposing his metaphysical and inner landscape to the scorching heat of these dreams, he forgets it was imagination.

III

Thinking is one of the most hazardous things in the world. It should be maintained and well treated every day because there's a difference between thinking that is hungry and the thinking that wants to devour. The hungry thoughts are to be fed with *knowledge*, but the *thoughts that want to devour, feast upon insanity*.

Thoughts are not ideas, but every idea is(or was) a thought. Thoughts can be assumed as a *prelude* to ideas (and actions.) That is the reason enough to tell us why they are shallow and deep at the same time. Thoughts are preludes, and thus it does not bear many fruits. Simultaneously, it is the first step toward the implementation of actions. Therefore it makes itself deep, profound, and essential. Your thoughts give meaning to your life, and when someone thinks more than much, obviously with sensible and valuable reasons, he becomes or tends to become a soul beyond morals because morality was once a *thought* too and the only weapon to shatter it is thinking itself.

A man who doesn't think should be considered dead. Thinking is the only disease that can cure death. When you have invented a new morality, it will live on— with or without you.

IV

The rendezvous of all questions is the point where the man faced with the nakedness of life meets with the errors of truth.

V

To become a Soul beyond morals, one must come to the agreement with himself that he'll never seek such knowledge that could never value his death.

VI

A man should only be in a box when he is dead. Don't confine yourself to the physical and psychic barriers, for they only delay the arrival of *thoughts*. No matter what the world says— death is the end for your mortal presence, but that doesn't necessarily mean your psychic presence will be vaporized too. You will continue to live as memories within the psyche of other people, and your thoughts will be inherited by those who had observed you carefully and metaphysically.

VII

Everything in this world is simple but the process of simplification is tantamount to knowledge, and knowledge is one of the most complex things to exist on the psychic plains of our minds. We don't even know what is knowledge and what is not—

VIII

Death is a part of life, and life is a part of death. We are all alchemists in our own way. Those who can't bear to take a Leap of Faith, to

jump from the moral attitudes, are condemned to be forgotten. The earth will eat both the souls of nature and souls beyond morals, but it will famish and relish more upon the souls of nature. Those who live according to nature are the ones who are destined to be devoured by it.
Death is not grief, but grief is death. Only those who *built* the earth and destroy their *hereafter* are afraid to die.

IX

What causes life is also a cause of beautiful death.

X

To most, resurrection is an Alchemy— *a dream for the soul beyond morals*, but it is entirely wrong. Resurrection is wished only by those who live according to the laws of nature because they've lived close to the *natural happenings of the world* resulting in them to hold onto those "happenings" and things that cannot go beyond the boundary of death or their morals. Ironically, resurrection is blasphemy by those who *involuntarily* believe in God's creation.
Those who live beyond morals dare to live beyond resurrections.

XI

Resurrection is craved by those who *think* they've something left undone. We must die knowing we've fulfilled our duties for we've no chances left for reiterations or redemptions.

XII

As I have said in my novella, Mendacity Of Death: *Redemption is not a chance but a choice*. And it is granted not by someone superior, but it is taken from us, by us. We seek redemption thinking it is a *fractural point* of our first life and the life after that fracture, and perhaps, we are gravely mistaken. It is not given to us from any external force but it is grown within our souls. We must venture into the past than think about the present. The past can never die, but the future can! And certainly, there is no present. What we call "*present*" is just the non-existing point between past and future. *Non-existing* in a sense that the past and the future are continuously moving... What we dub to be "present" is just a moment where the past and the future meet, and the moment may exist endlessly, which is not true because it can't exist more back in the past or more forward to the future.

XIII

I said earlier that *the past can never die, but the future can...* The past is already there, you cannot *kill* it, but the future is *uncertain.* The past is what ensures our redemption and our decision to redeem ourselves. To reject the morality of the past is not redemption, but to correct and go beyond the boundaries of it is... The souls beyond morals don't seek redemption because they have already redeemed themselves the moment they jumped from the summits of *defective* moralities. Rather than climbing the tallest mountains, the souls beyond morals dive into the deepest oceans.

XIV

Seeing my contemporaries, I can assure myself that there will rise poets of newer generations who will write everything about grief except the ways to cope with it. Also, some poets will write everything about love except its remedy. The time is in sight when women will write about freedom and men will write about love, and it won't be ironic anymore.

XV

Something that seems 'calculable' doesn't mean it's easy to interpret. Likewise, *we exist for reasons we can calculate, but can never interpret* as we are bounded by our morals, no matter how fickle or great. Thus, there must exist a *warning* when we cross this distorting boundary i.e. our senses and individualism. Many philosophers have written their philosophy keeping the "I", either in their statements or in the silent form in those statements driven solely by perspectives and perceptions.

XVI

To create a new standardized morality, *the soul must be free from self-evaluations.* You cannot trust your senses if they are *made functional by others.* Being born has no role and neither is proportional to the procedure to hereditary— being conscious and genuinely conscious without being driven by conclusions of others is... Hereditary is not passing of 'folklores', but of adding new essences and in rare cases, creating new relevant *stories.*

XVII

Behind all logic, there stands evaluation, but in many cases, behind all truths, there stand unclear conclusions. Also, behind all evaluation stands logic but behind conjectures stand no truths.

XVIII

To be free is to be redeemed, and never the world of deeper intelligence open to those who are not daring explorers. Such a world of insights doesn't demand earthly sacrifices— it has its gates open only to those formidable ones who sacrifice intellectual thoughts. Because to learn more, you must consider yourself the greatest fool.

XIX

The greatest charm of theories is not of them being honest but the fact that they might be *refutable*. Many theories and philosophies are based upon the philosophers' will to impose their powers upon certai*n truths...* And once a mortal with a *subtler* mind discovers the specific flaws of perspectivism in such theories, he becomes an infant to Soul Beyond Morals because what we see is not the truth but our perceptions. For example, in love: the grotesque of all faces are considered beautiful to the lovers' eyes.

XX

Love is either a clear complexity or a complex clarity.

greatest fool.

XV

The greatest charm of the [illegible] is not [illegible] bringing [illegible] out the fact that [illegible] of the [illegible] and [illegible] power [illegible] Surely the specific [illegible] becomes [illegible] to Scott [illegible] the [illegible] all [illegible] considered [illegible]

[illegible]

BIBLIOGRAPHY

Poe, E. A. **Israfel.** Poems. Complete Stories and Poems of Edgar Allan Poe. Doubleday Publishers, Aug 15, 1984

OTHER WORK BY AL MINAR M. REZA INCLUDES:

Mendacity Of Death - *A Novella*

Printed by Libri Plureos GmbH in Hamburg, Germany